Writerly
PAPERIE

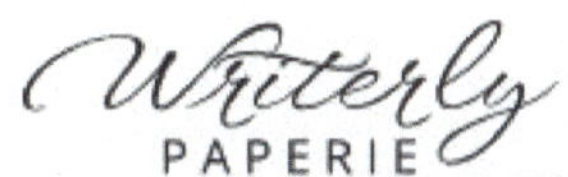

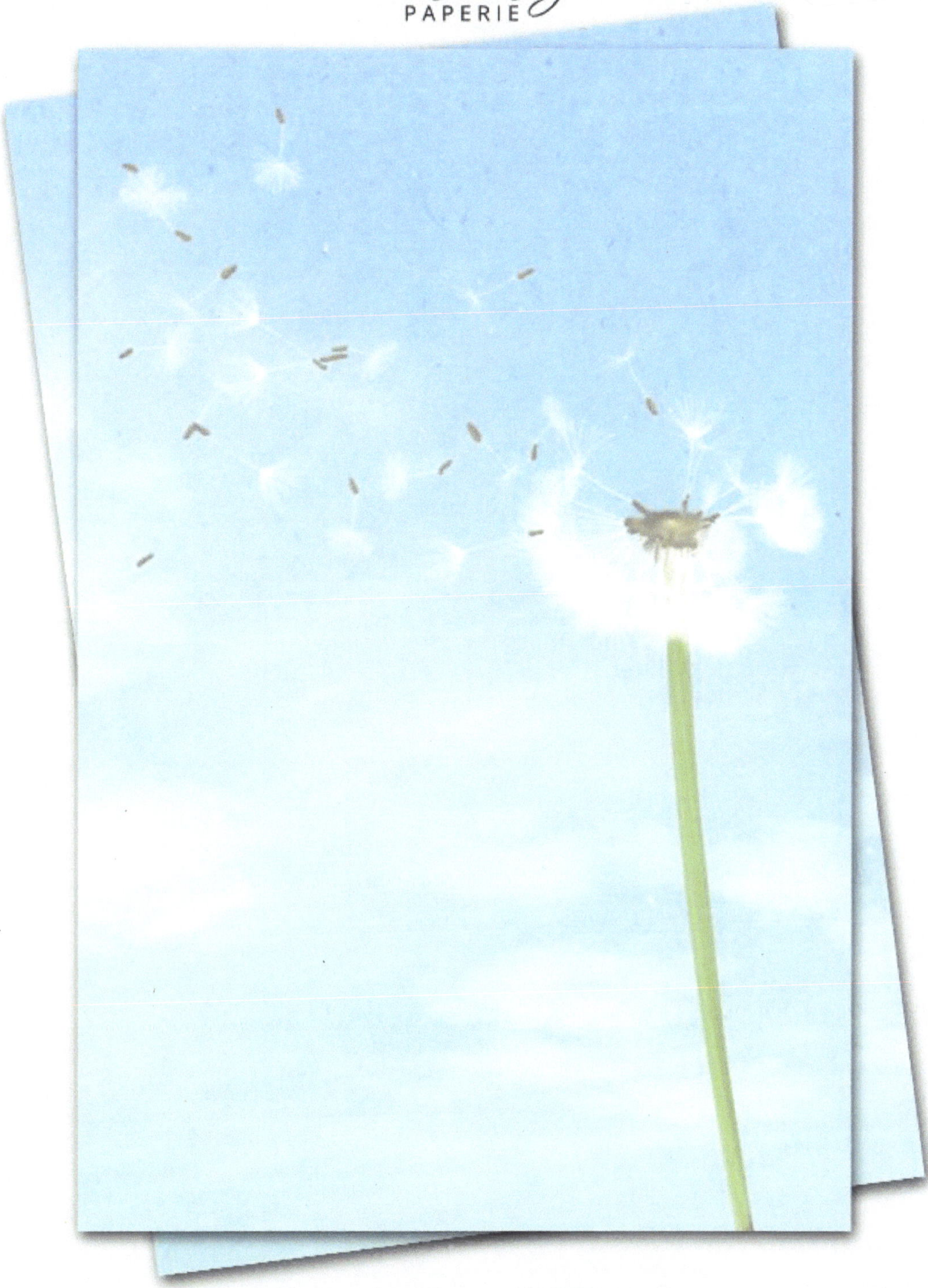

Dandelion Clouds

STATIONERY PAPER

25 SHEETS | 5.5" x 8.5" | Half-Letter Size Paper | Simply Cut Out & Use

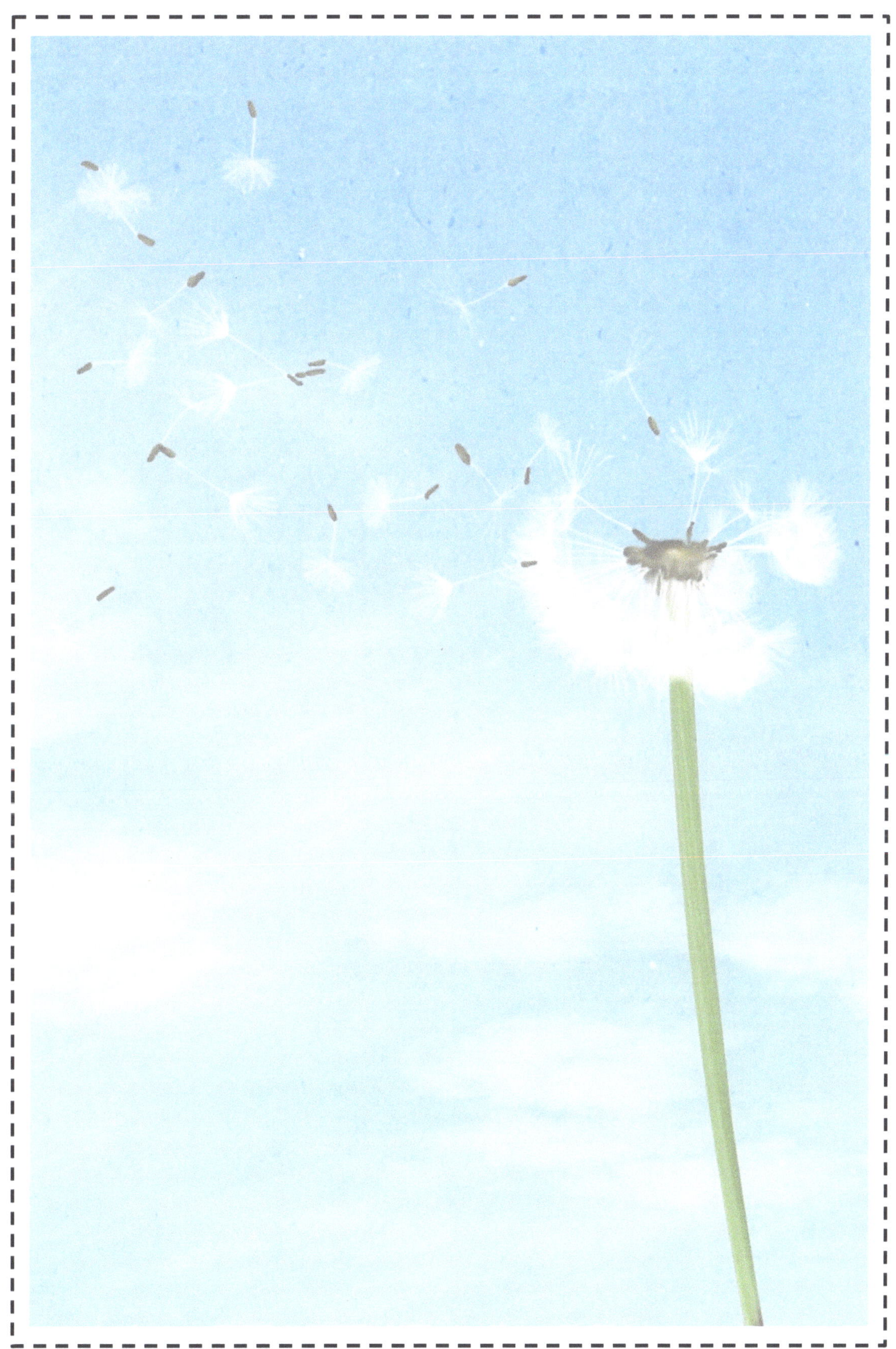

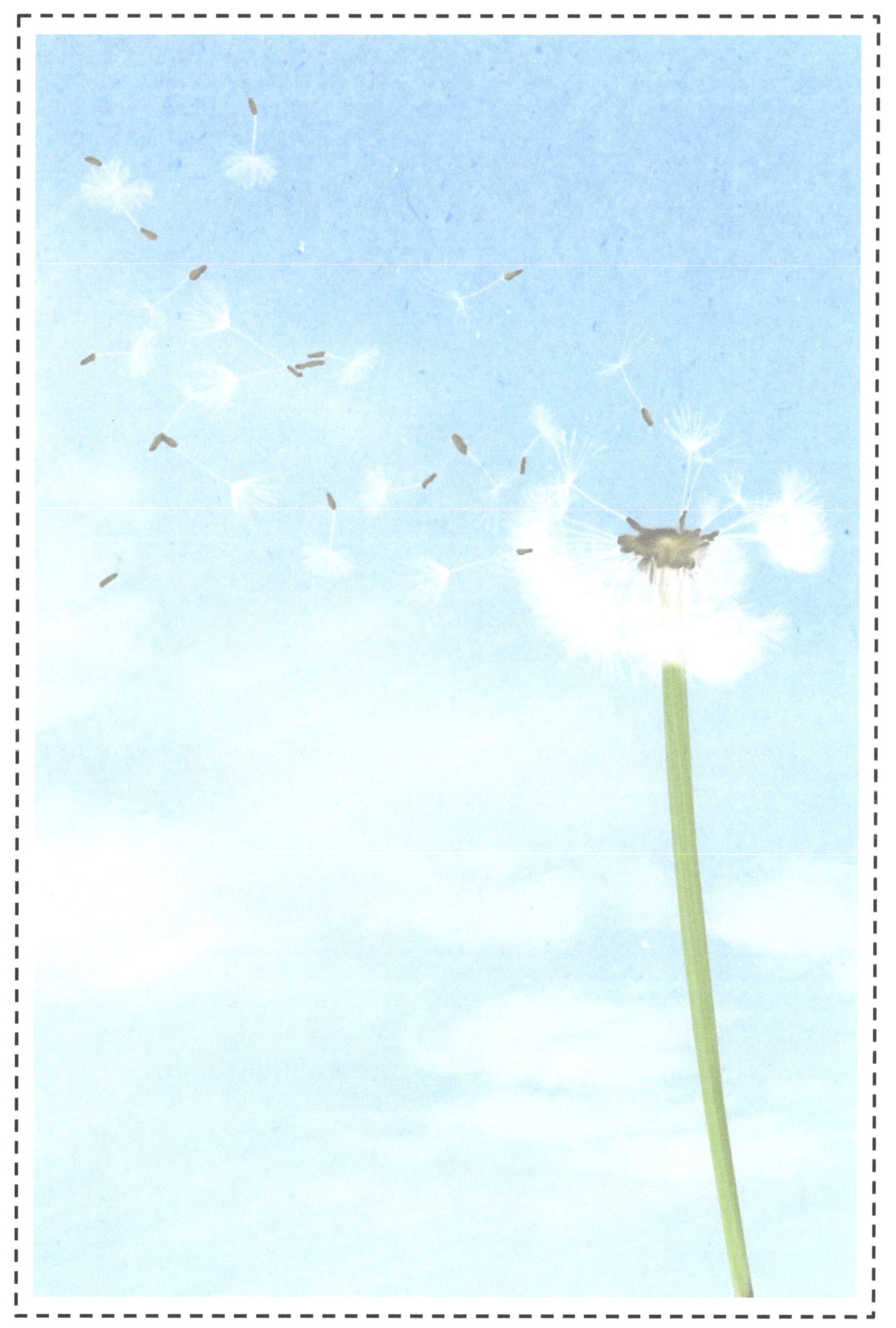

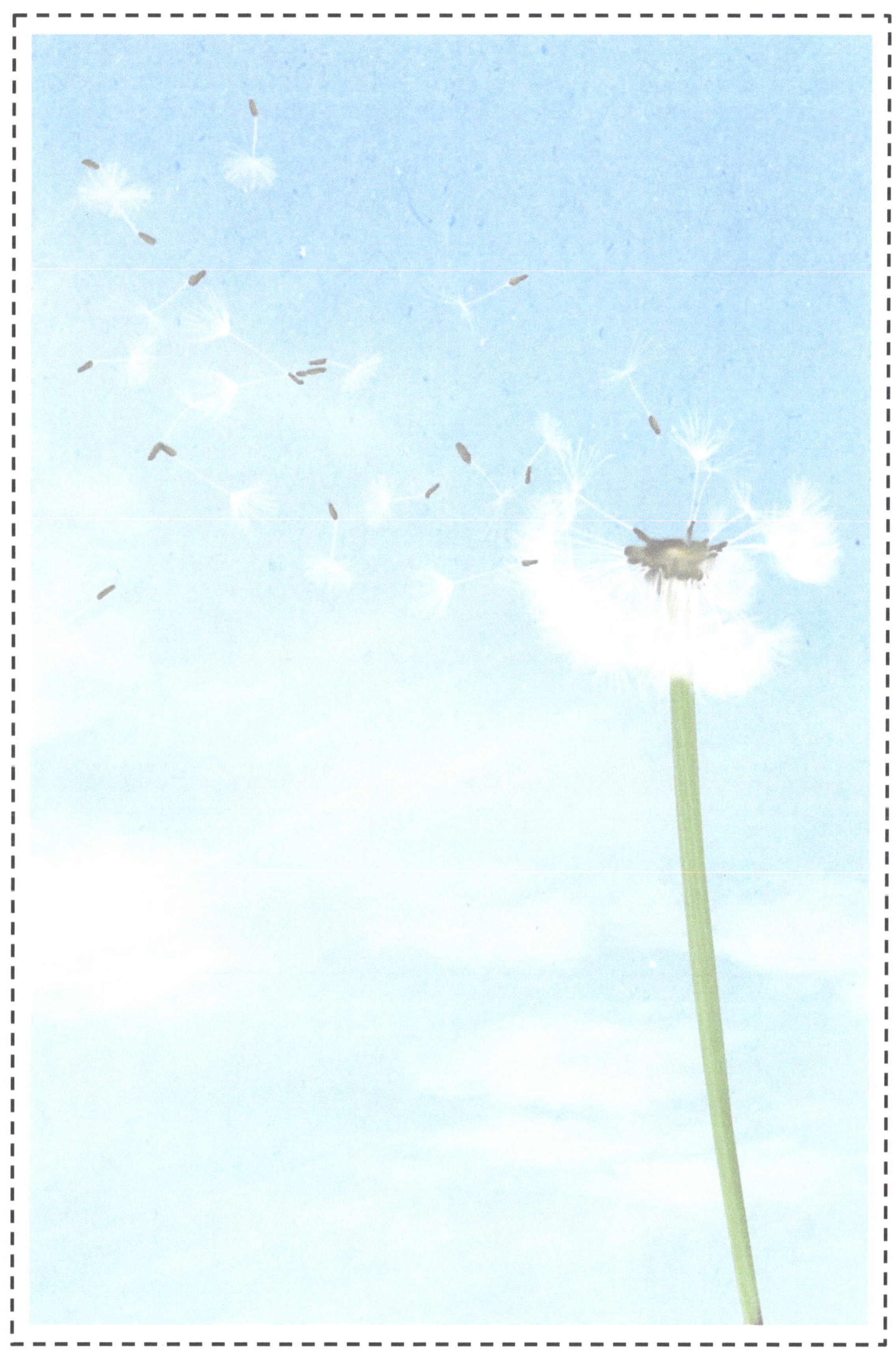

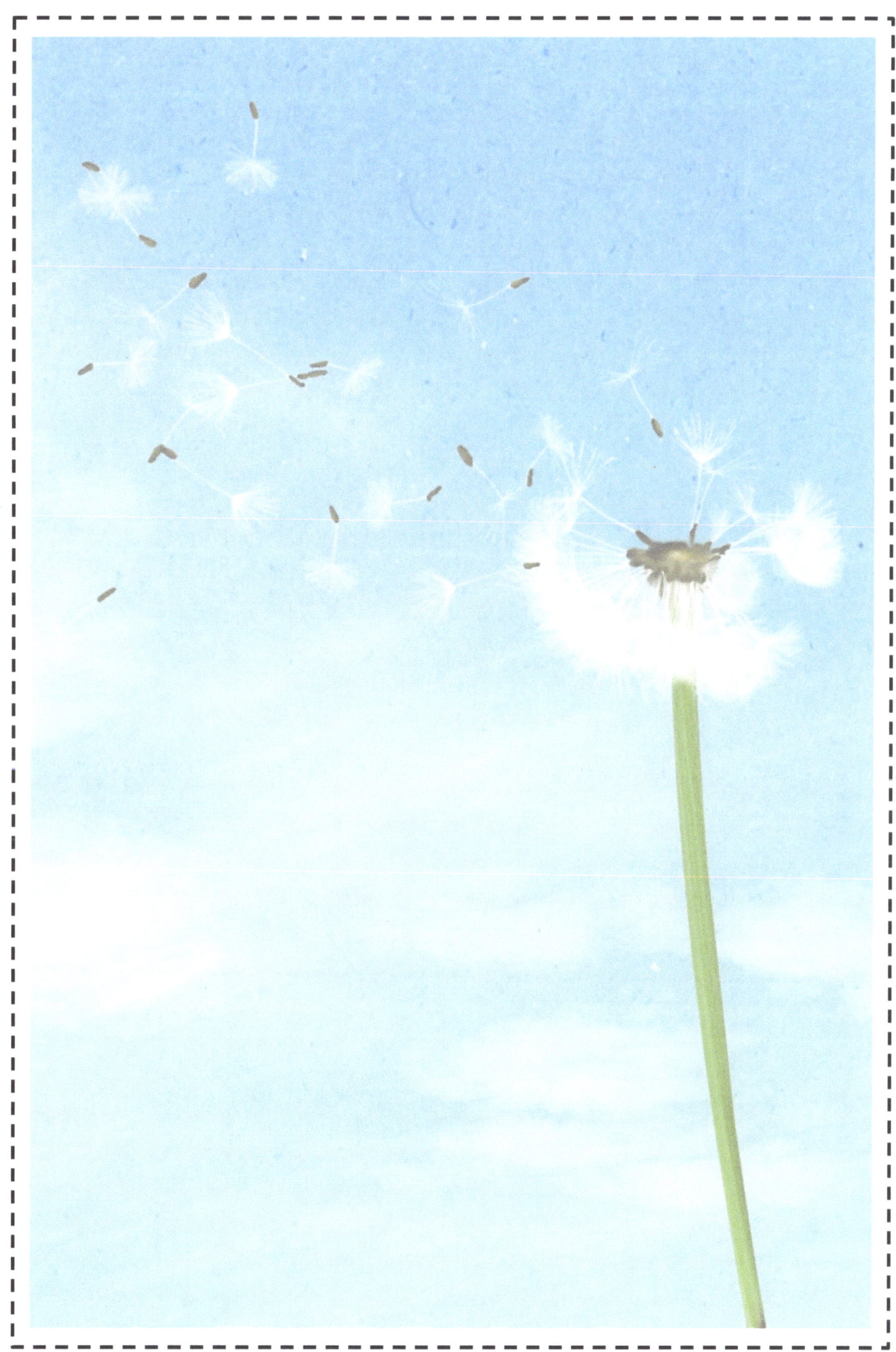

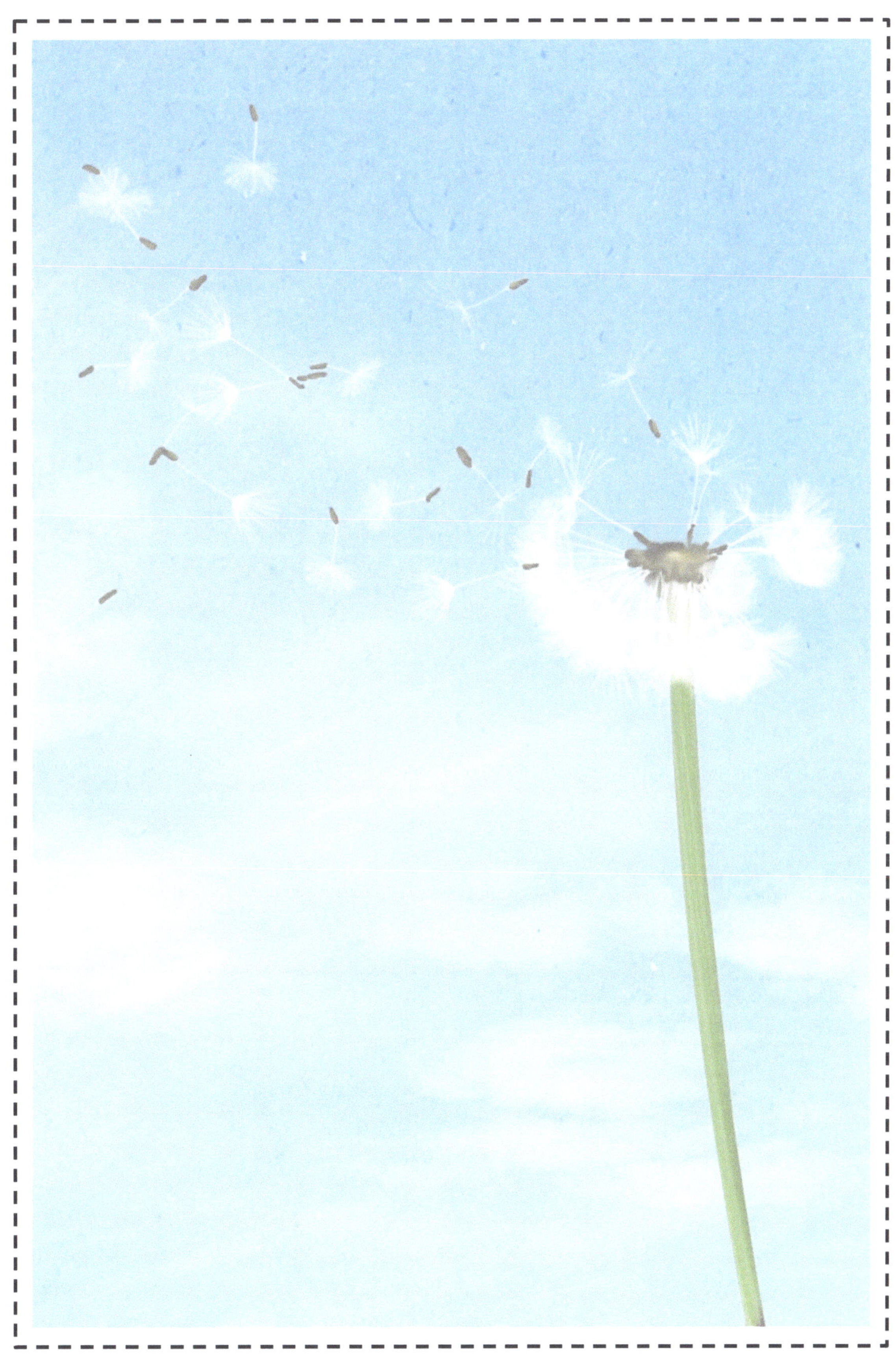

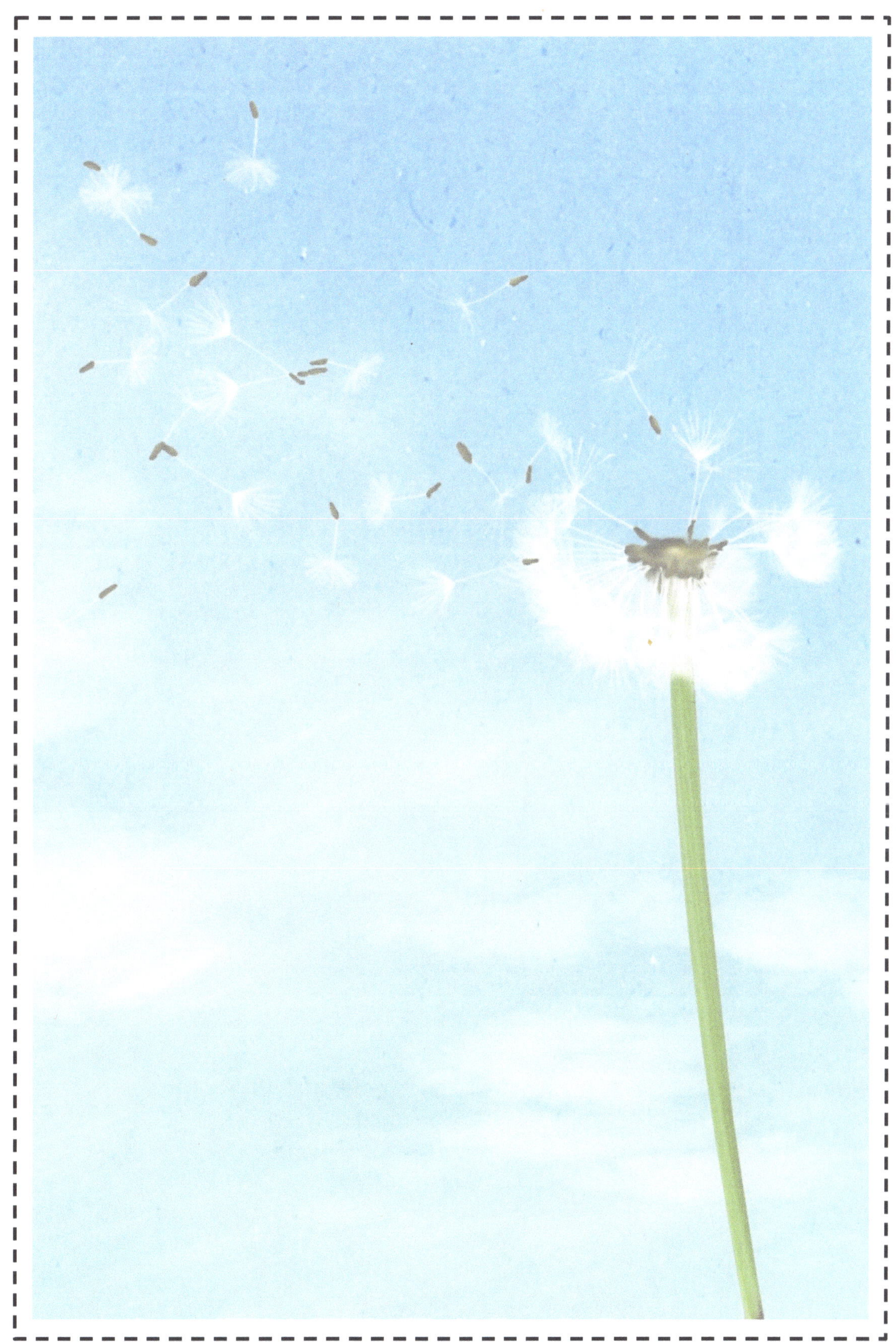

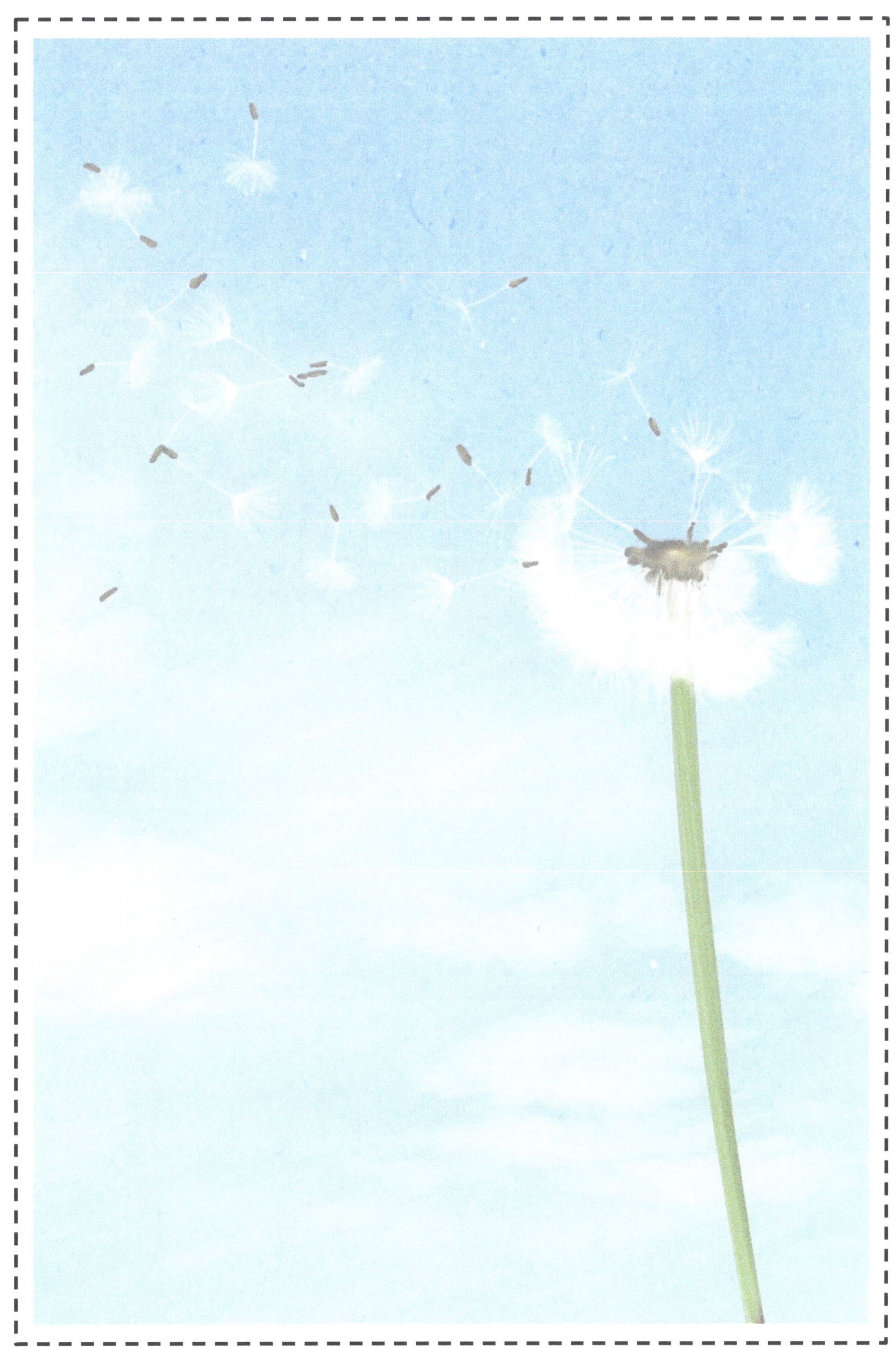

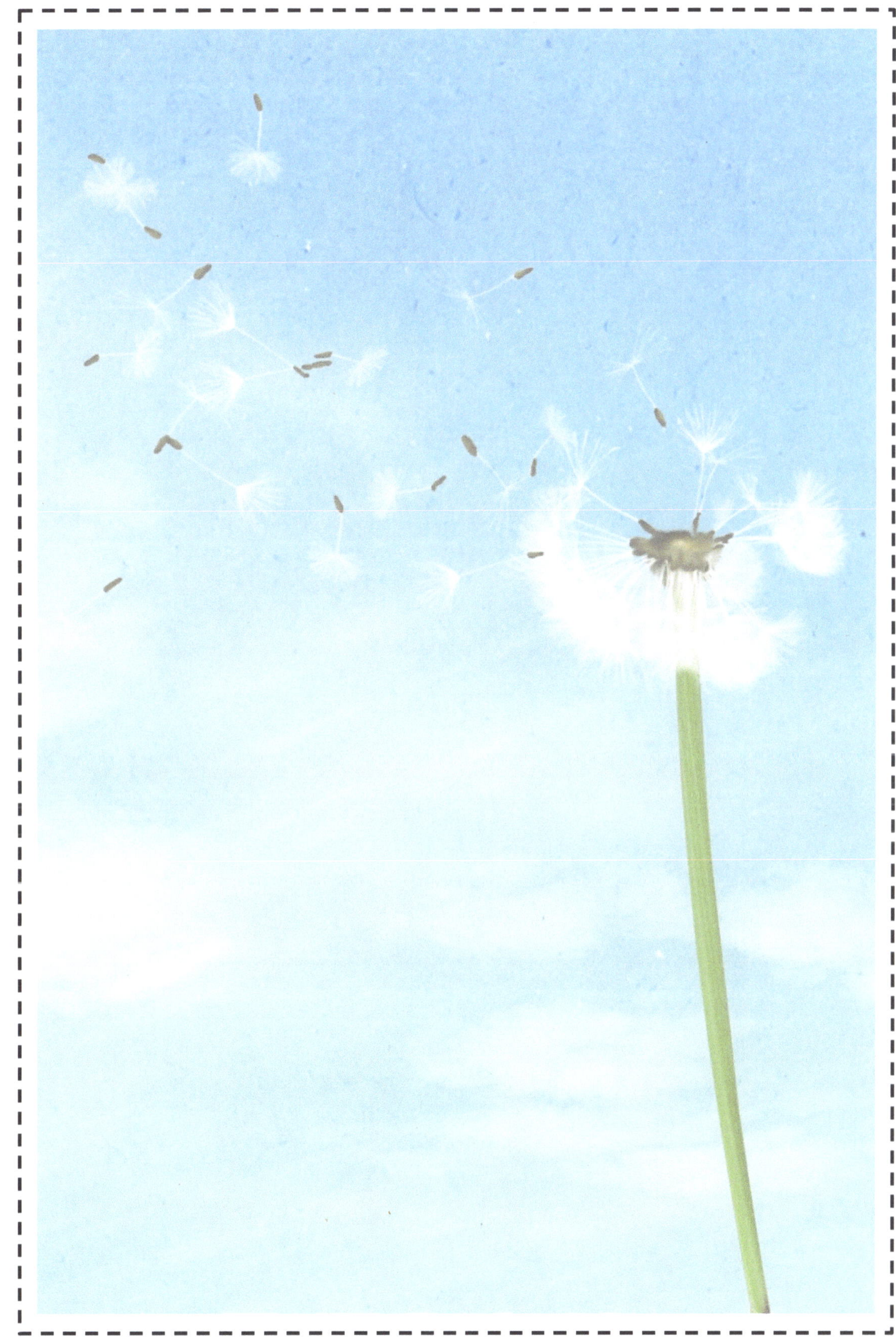

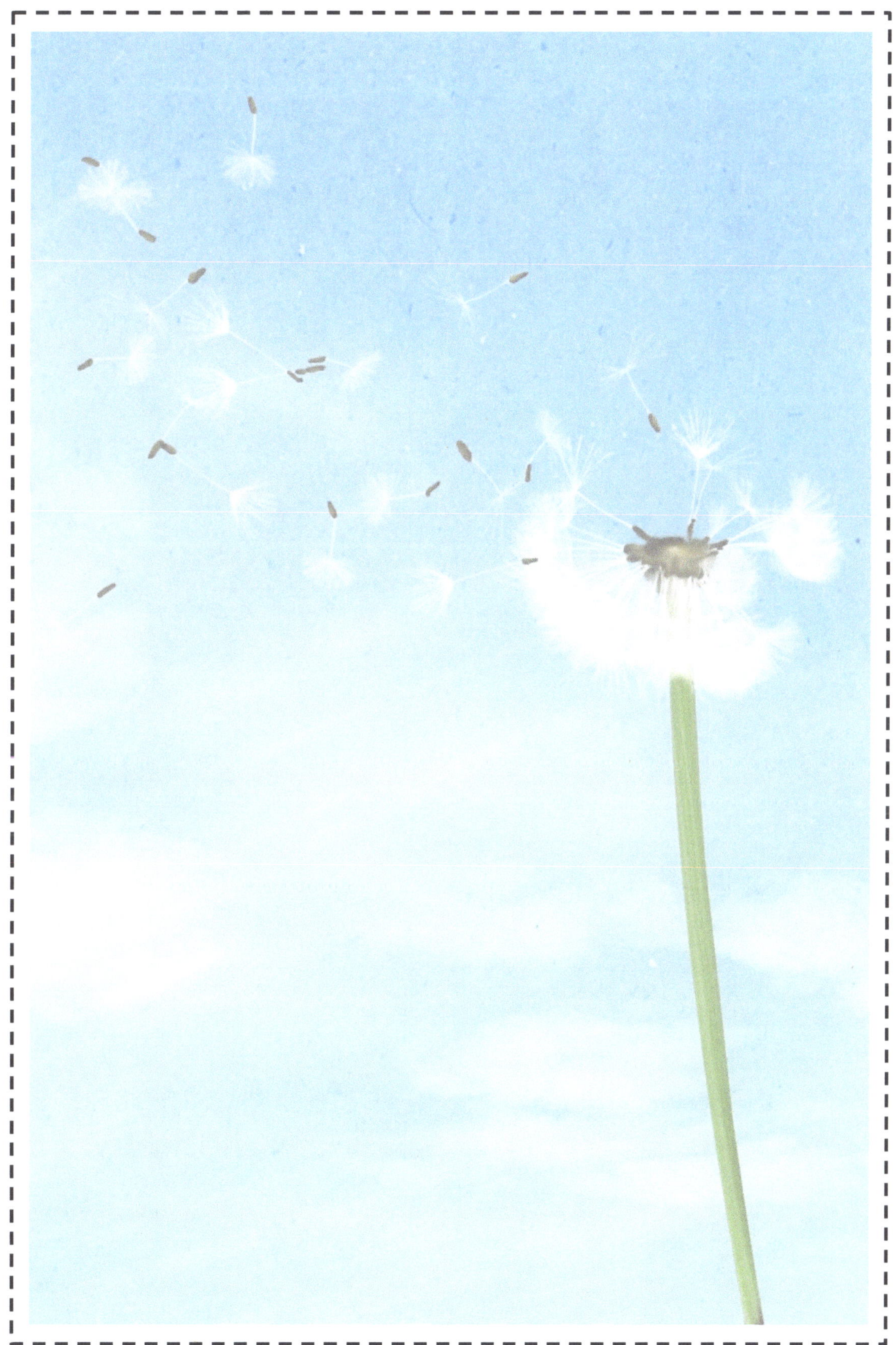

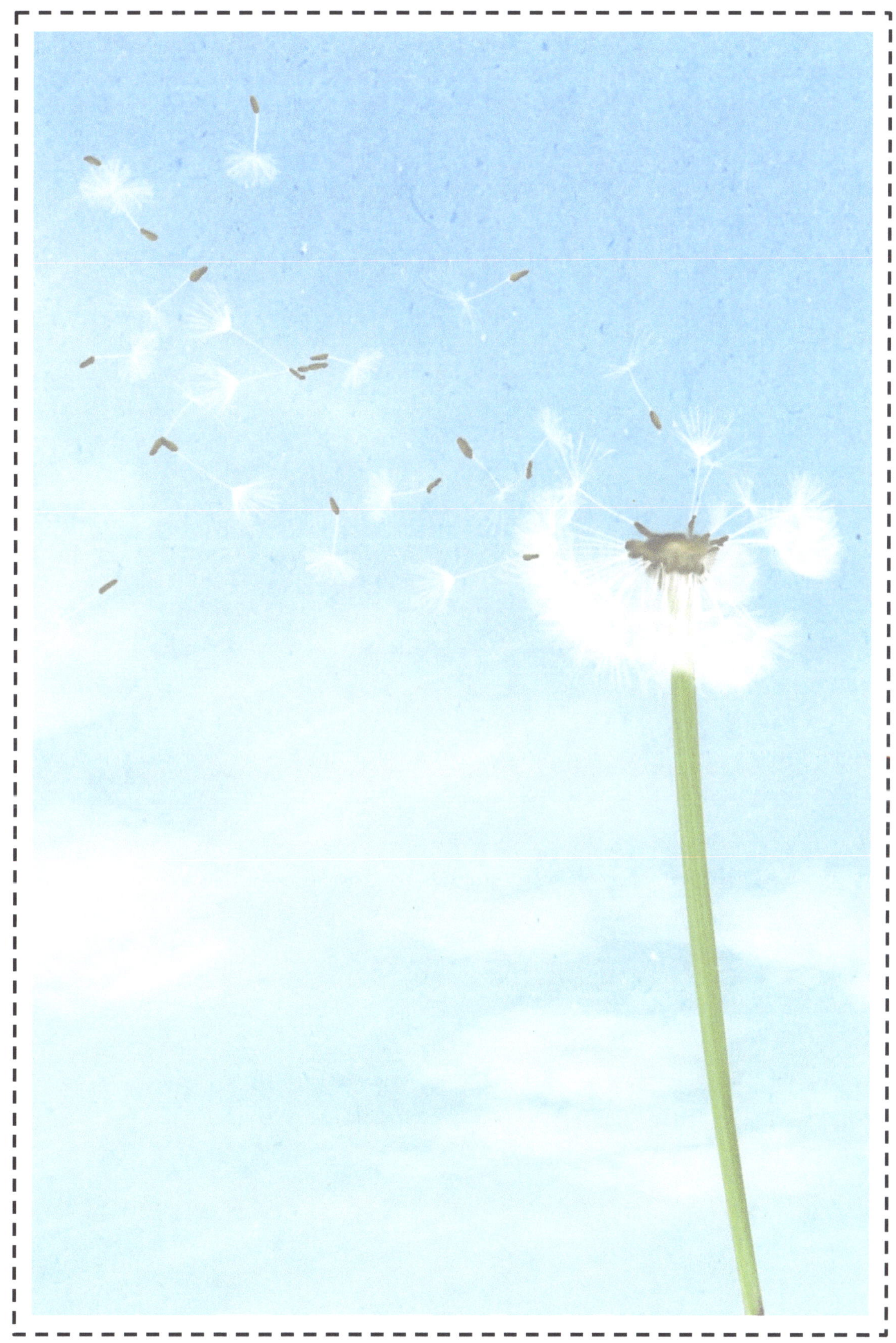

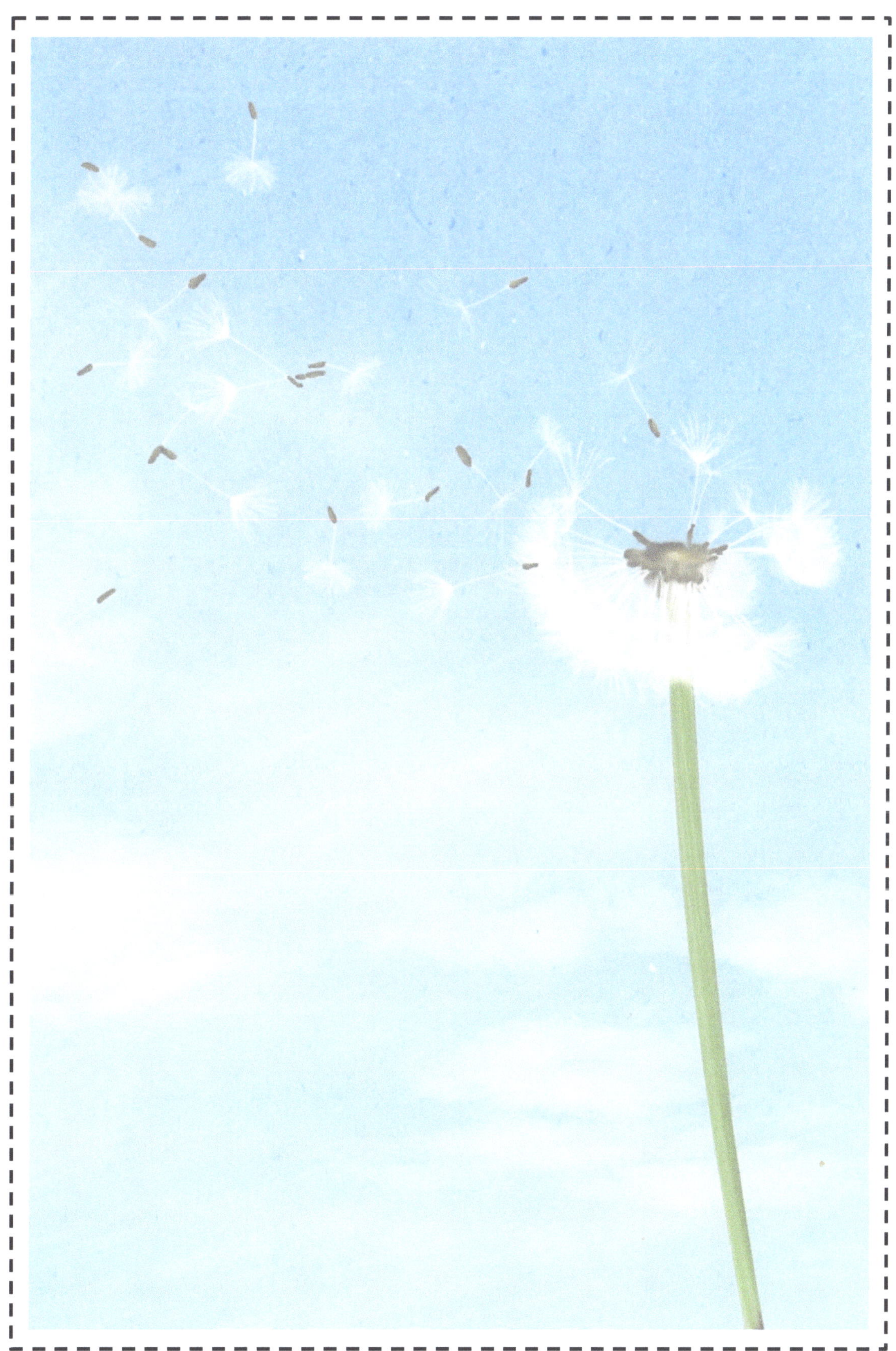

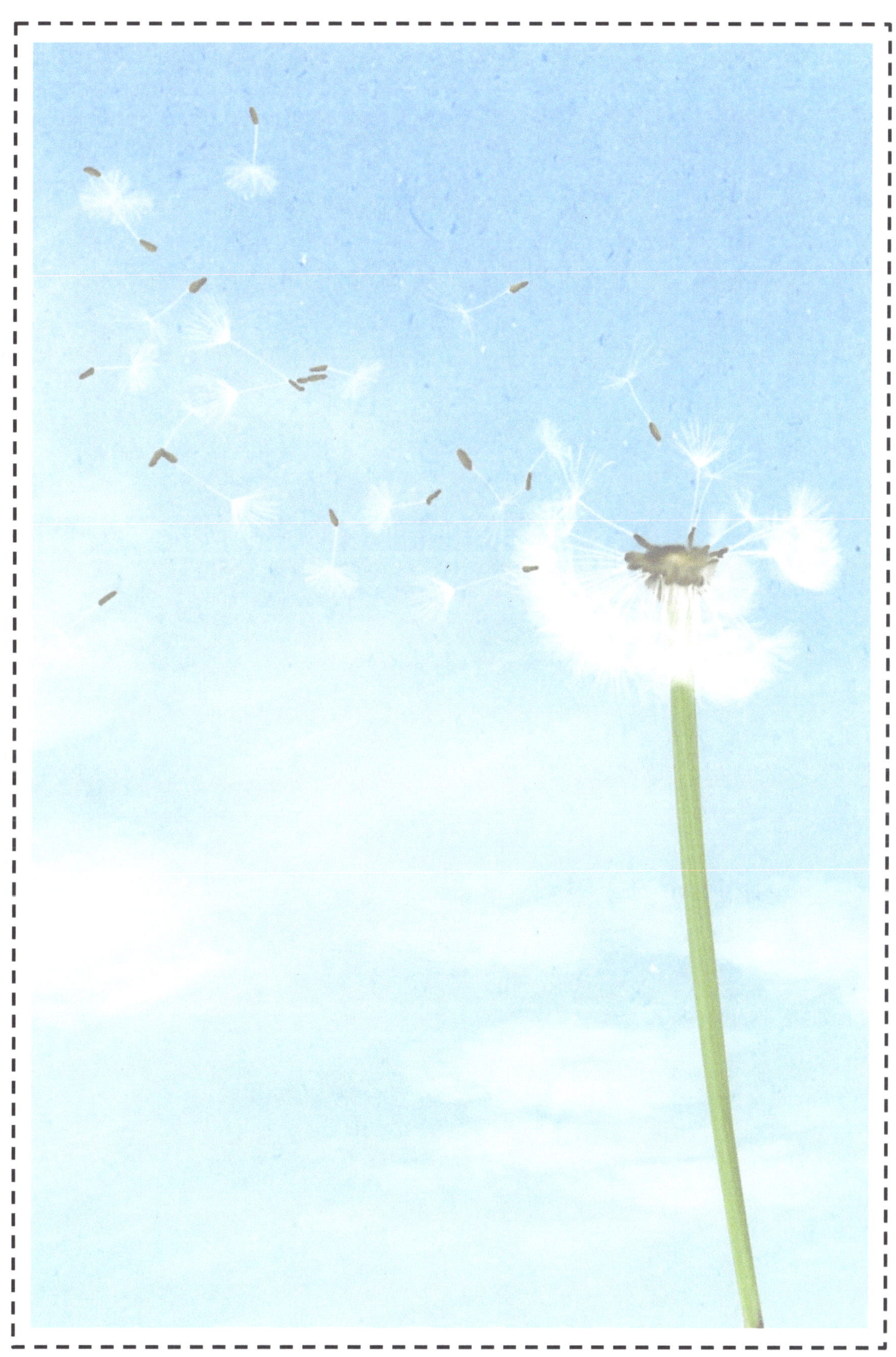

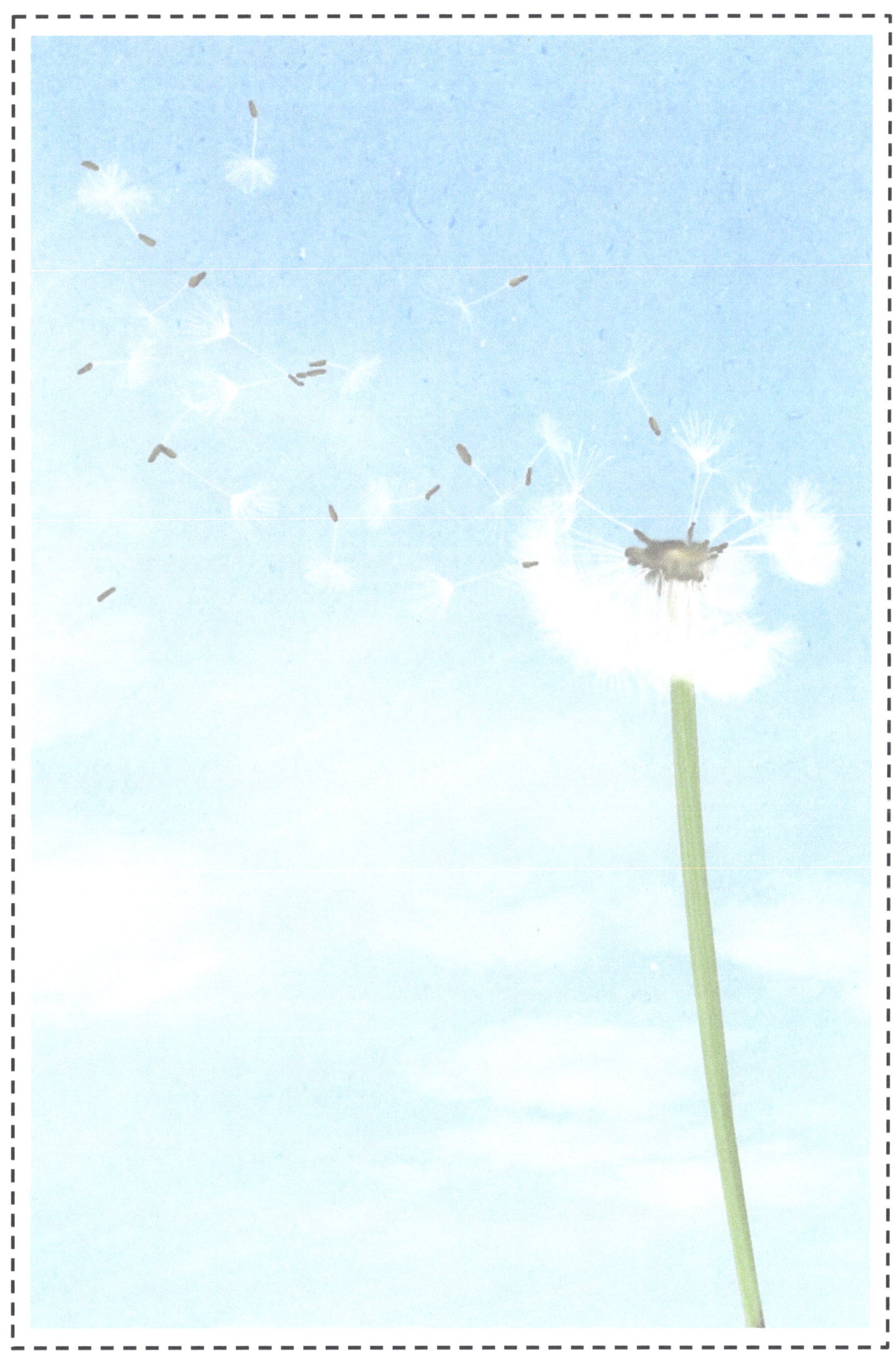

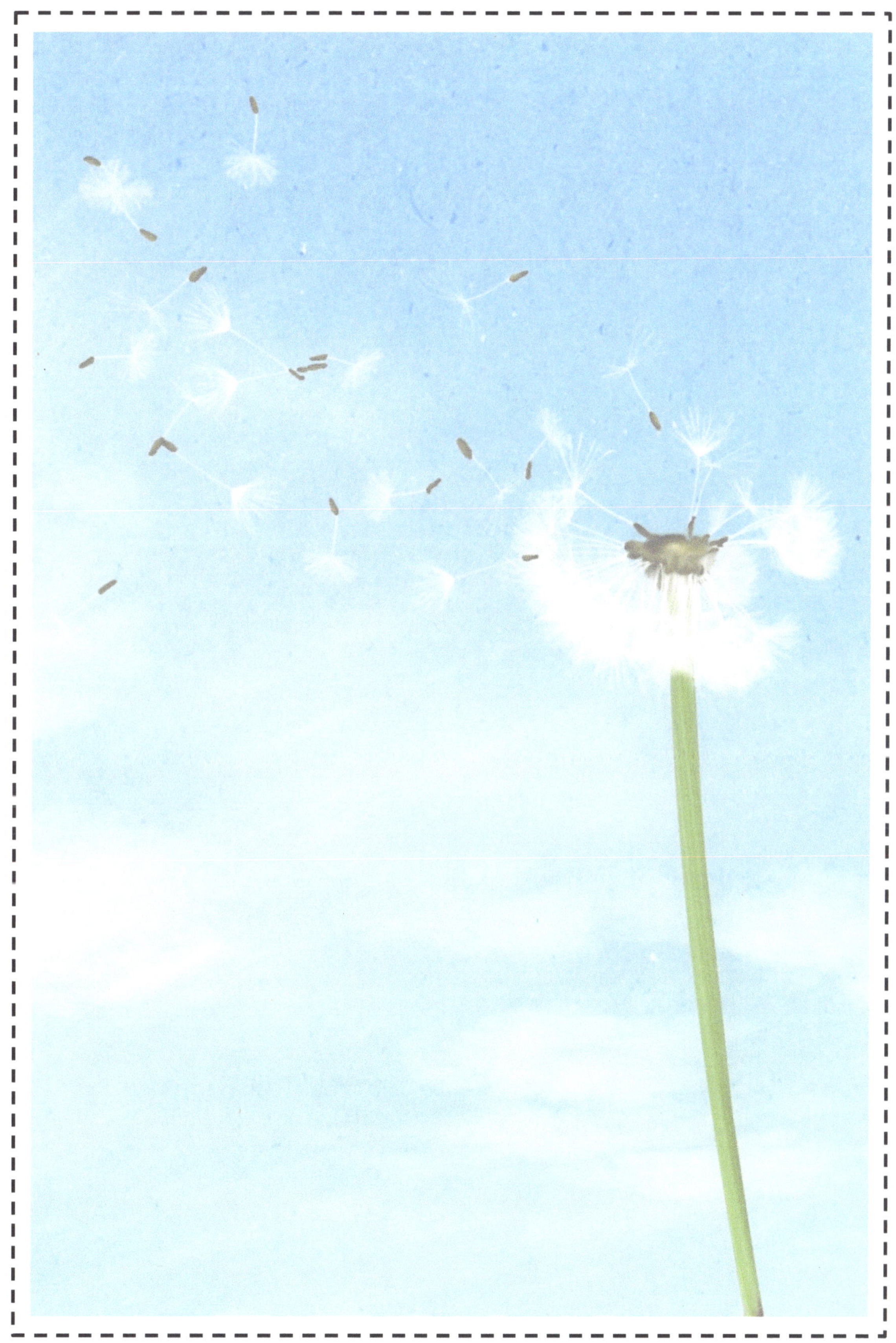

Simply Cut Out & Use

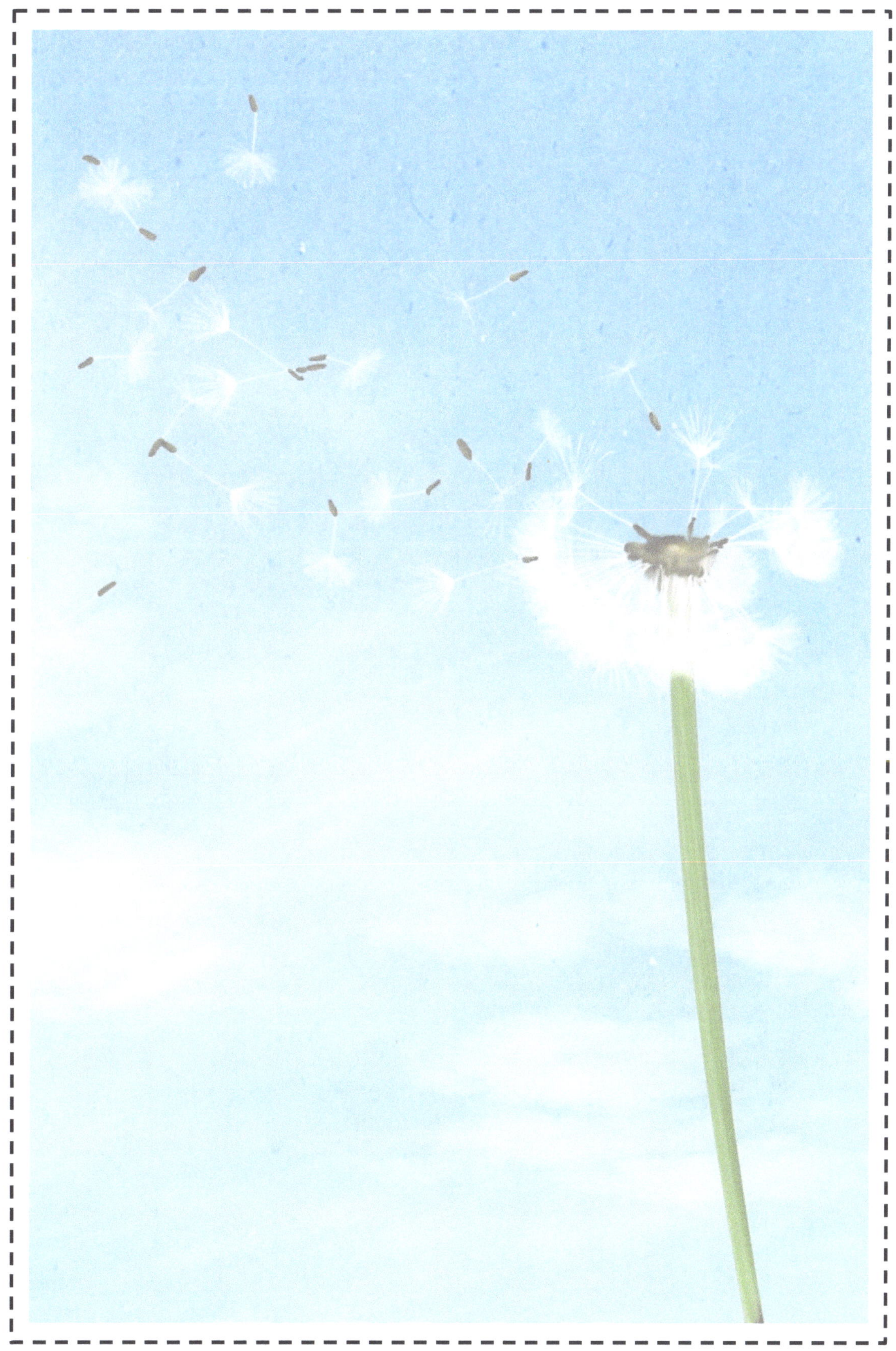

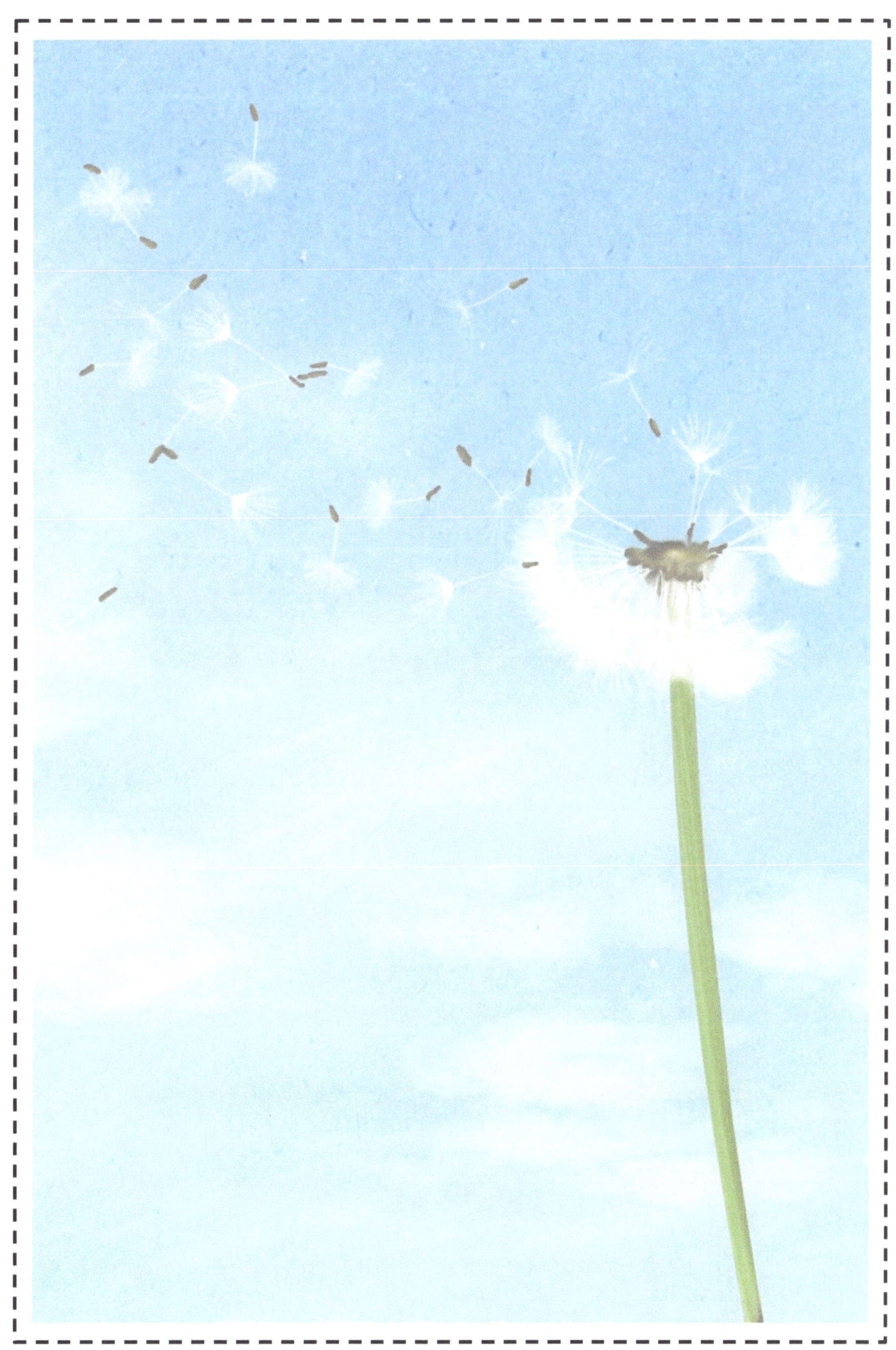

Simply Cut Out & Use

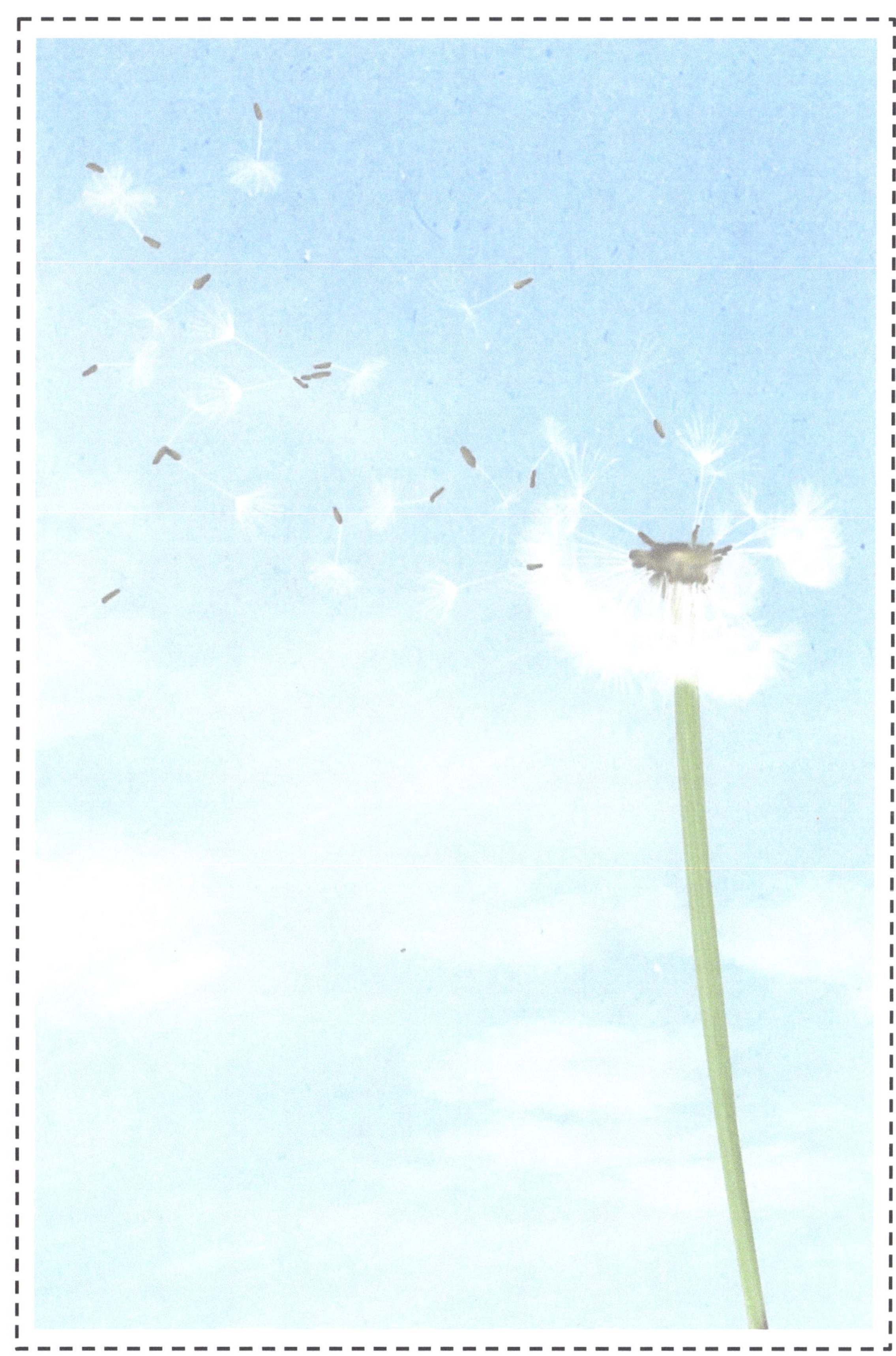

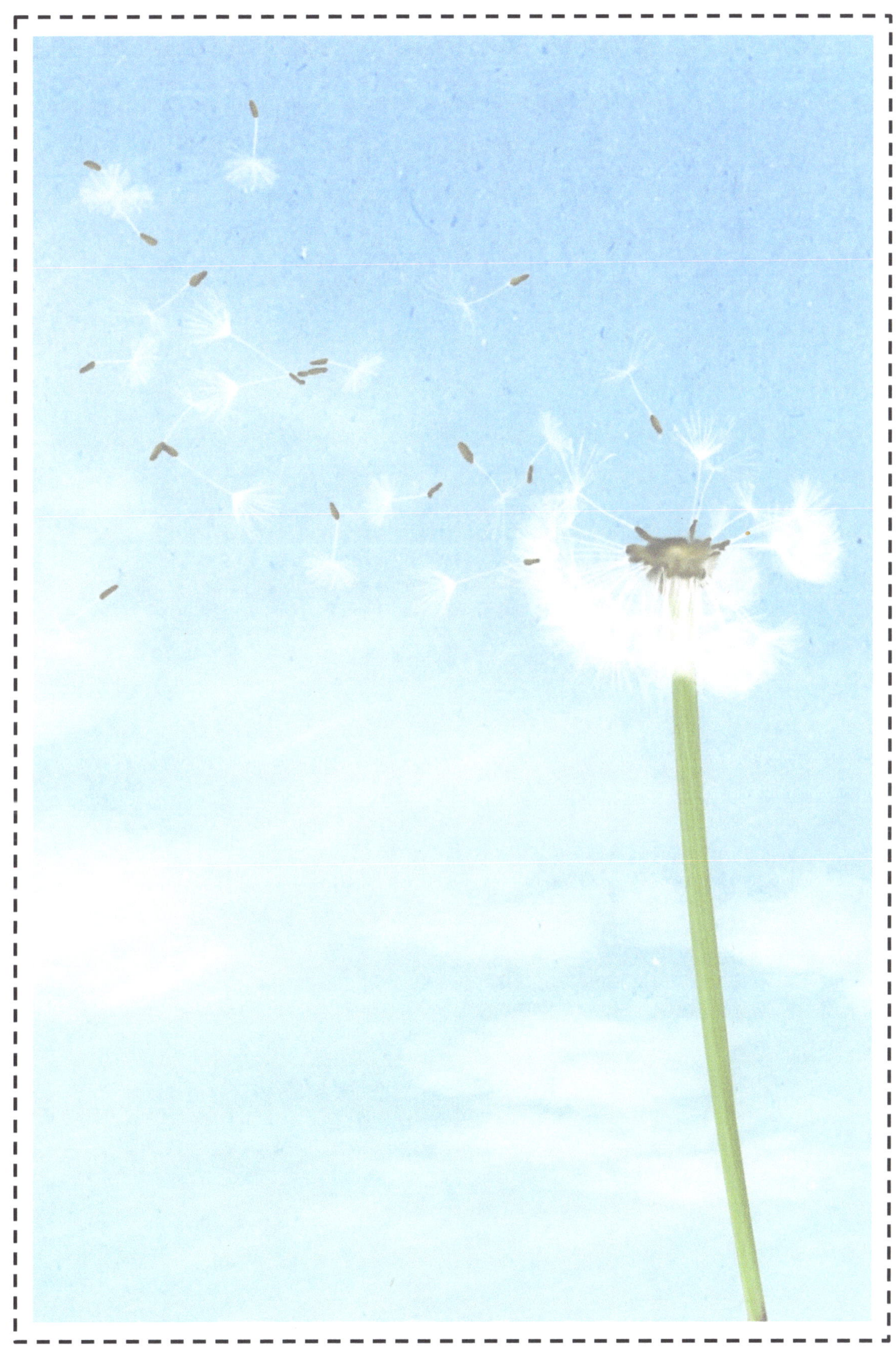

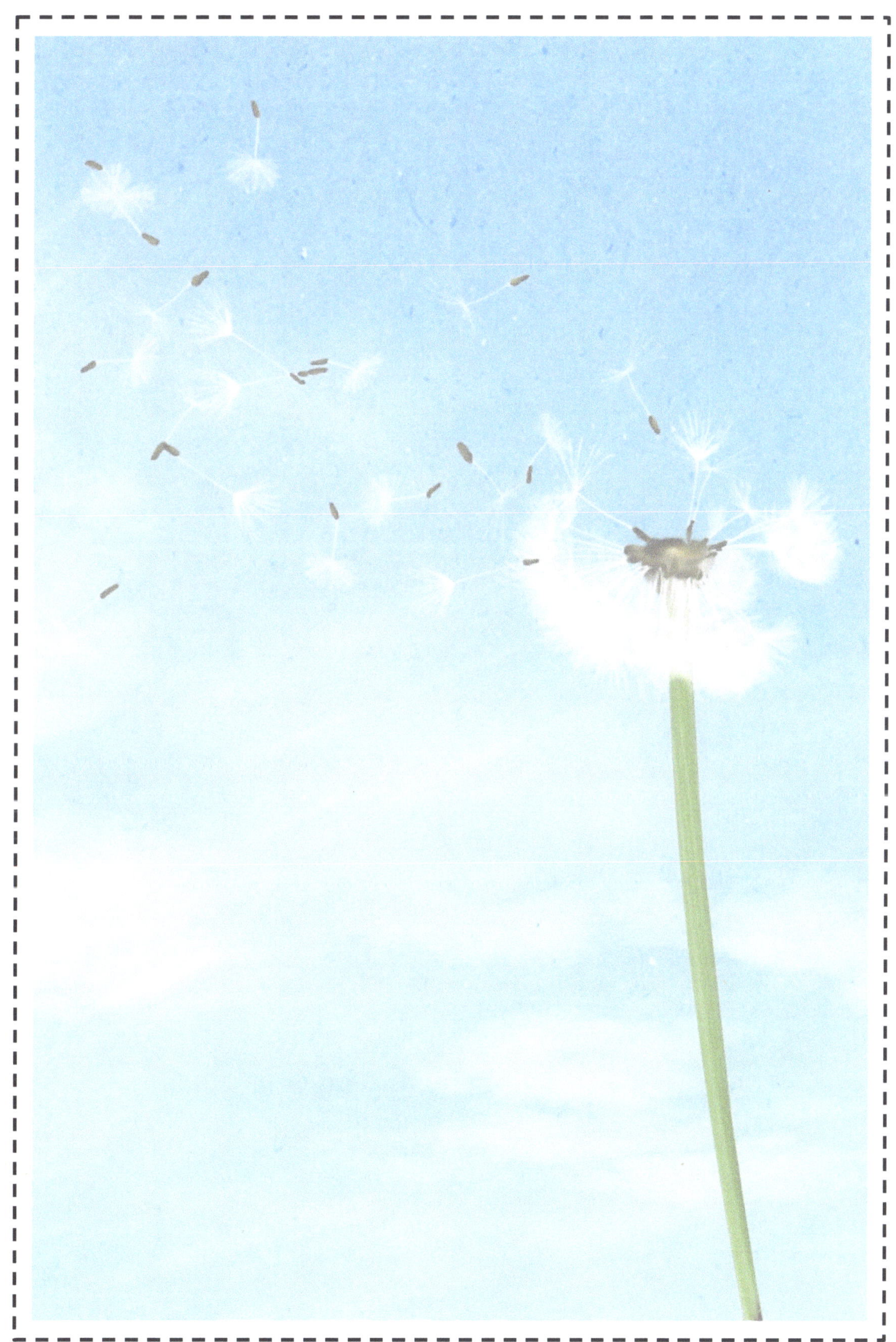

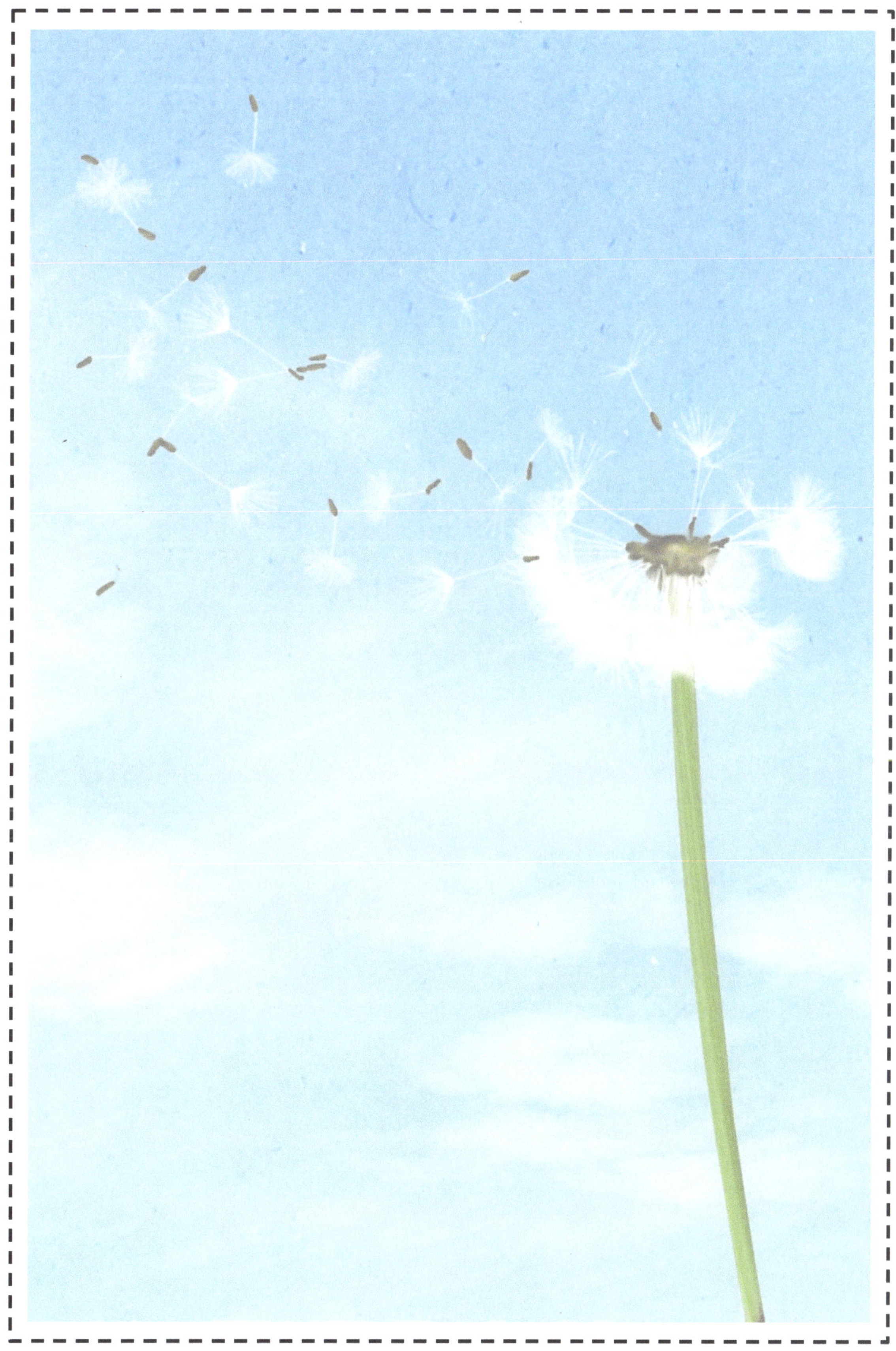

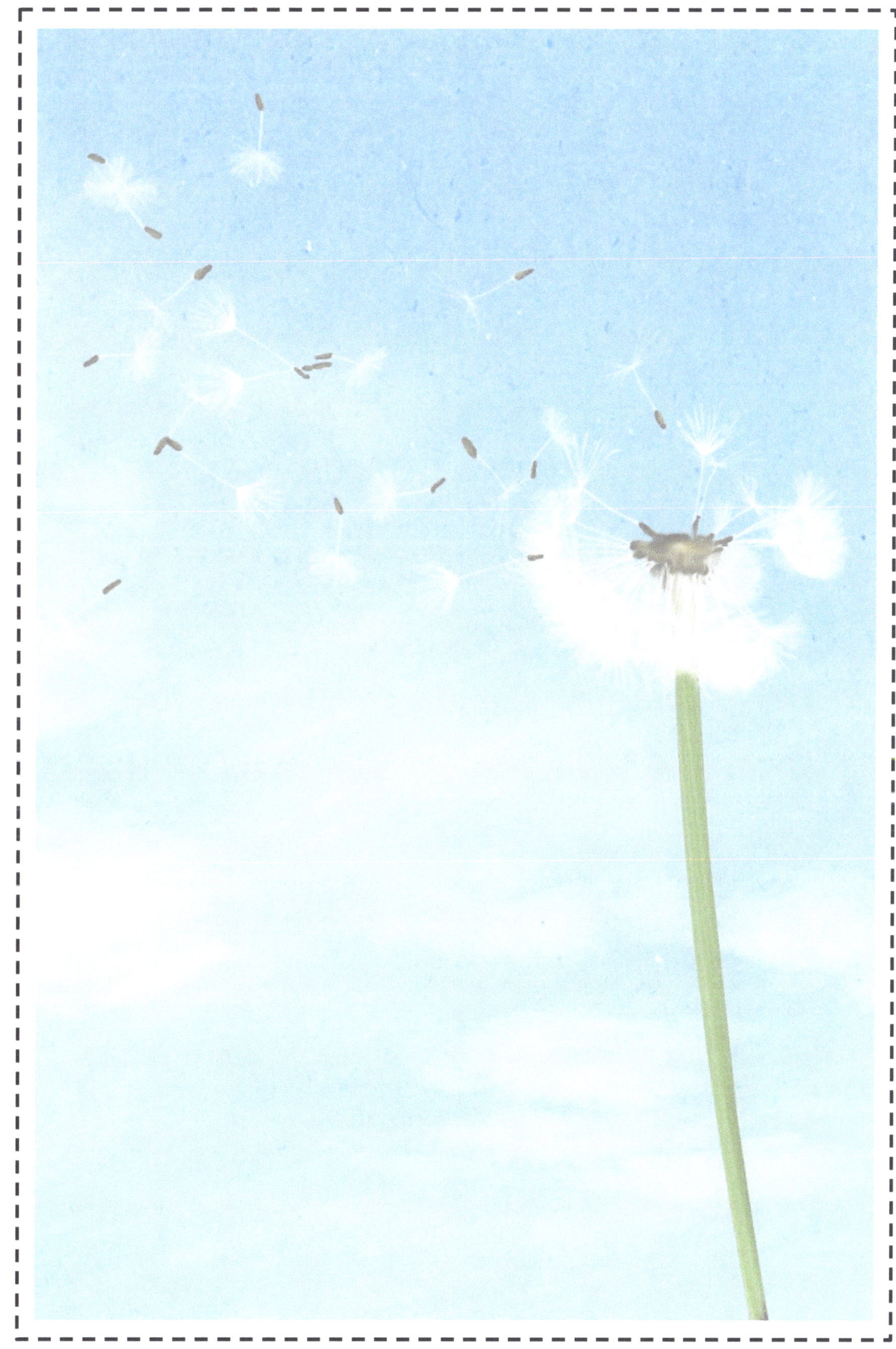

Simply Cut Out & Use

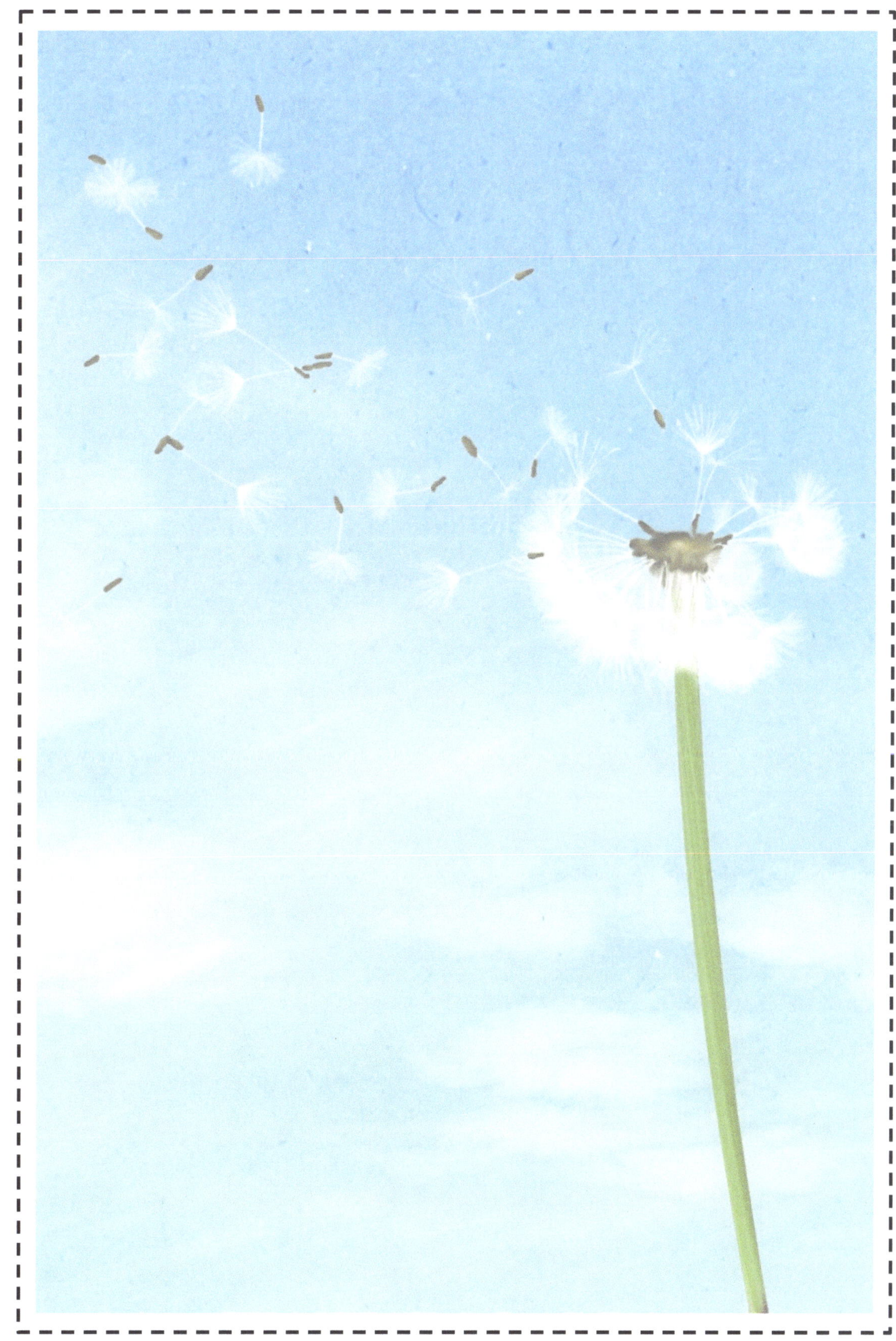

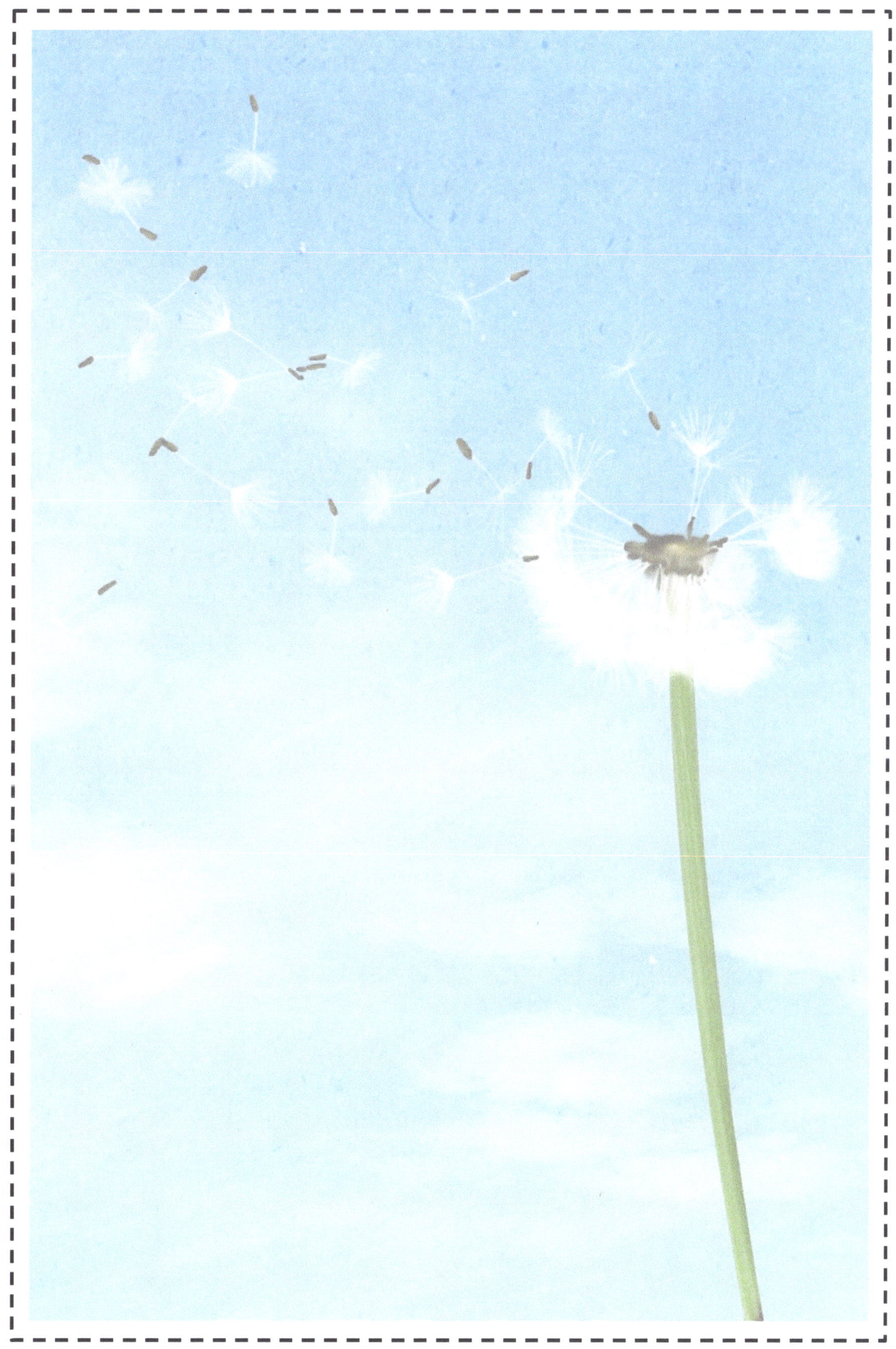

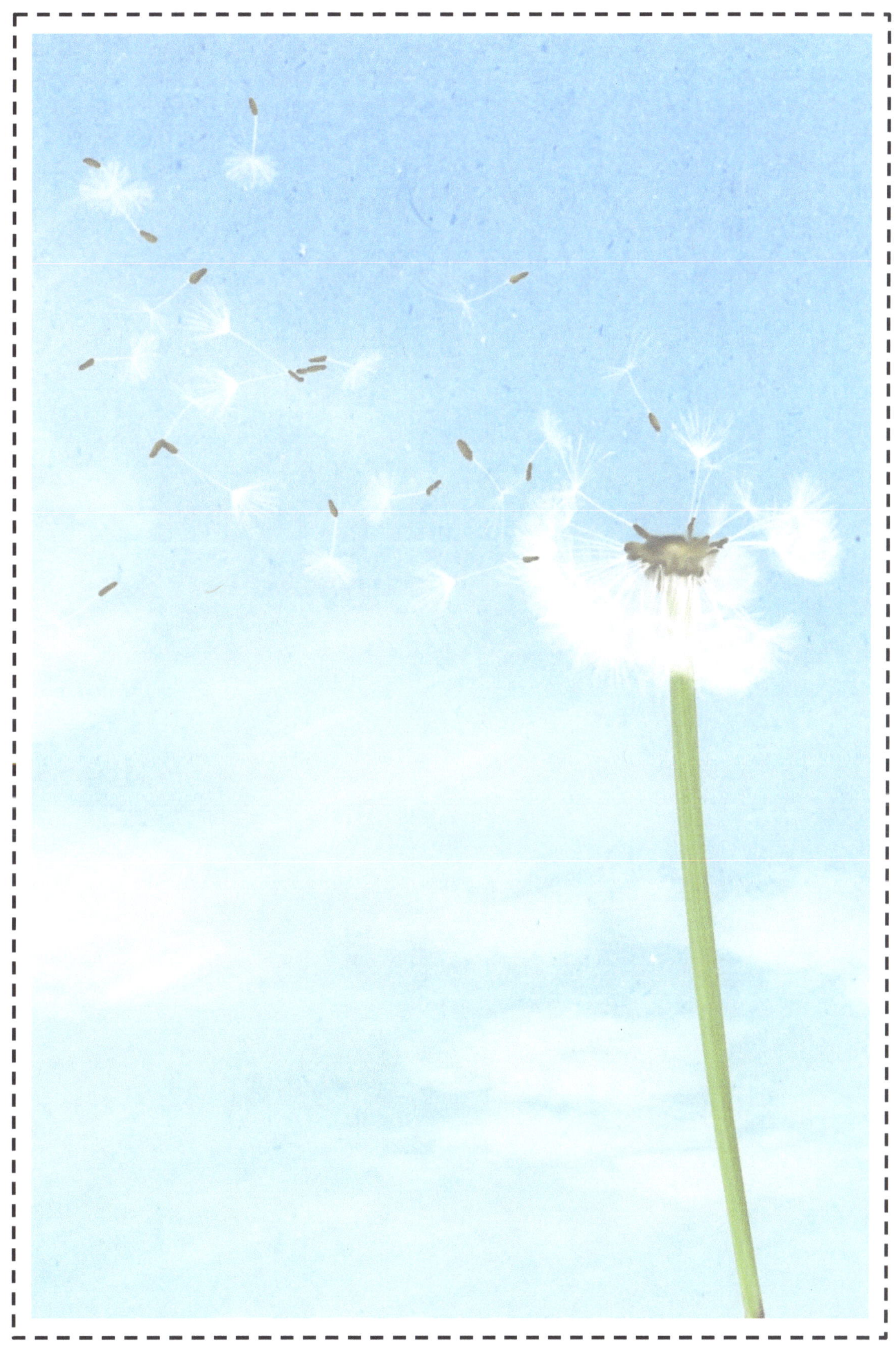

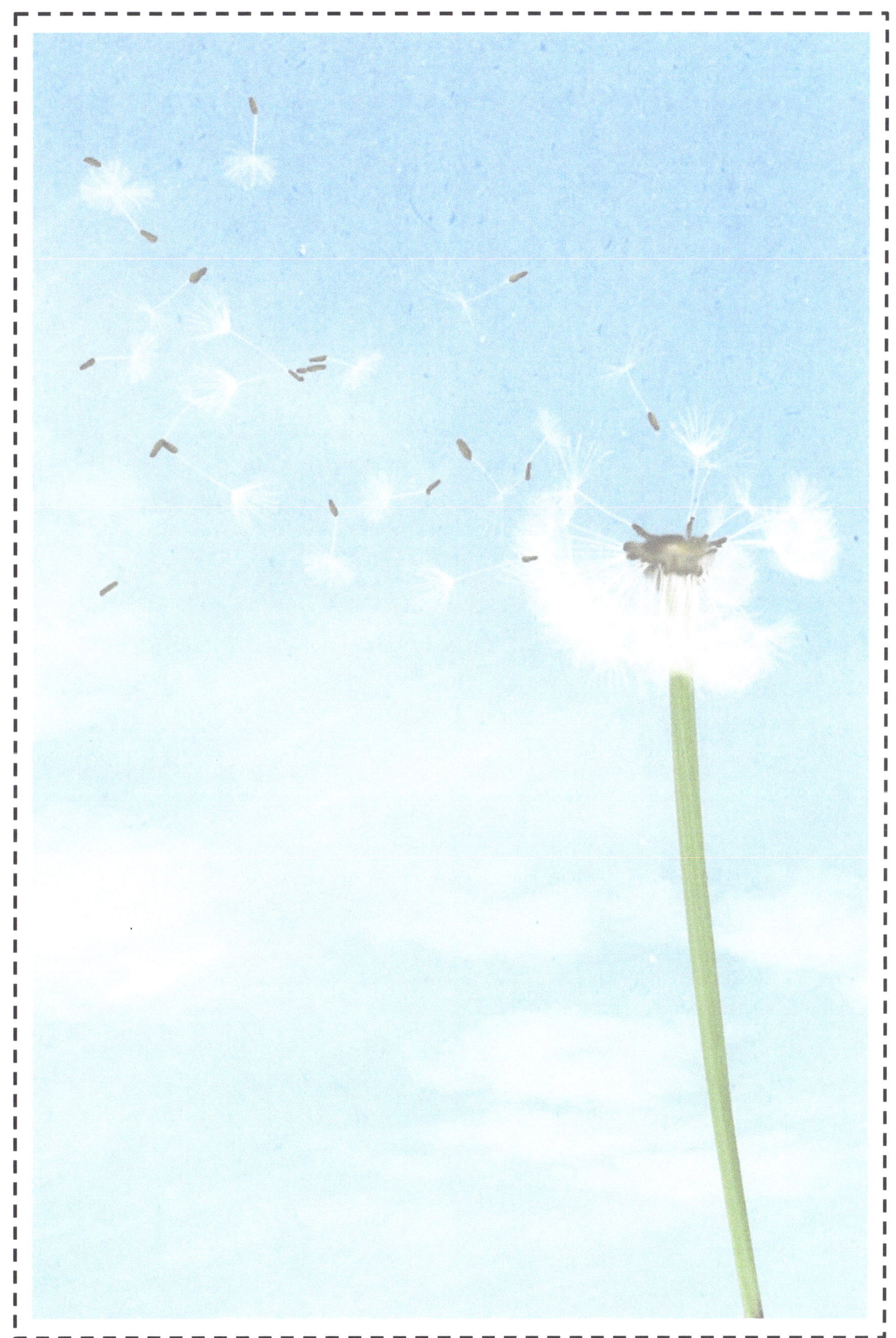